How to Draw Funny Faces For Kids

Author Tony R. Smith

Original Picture

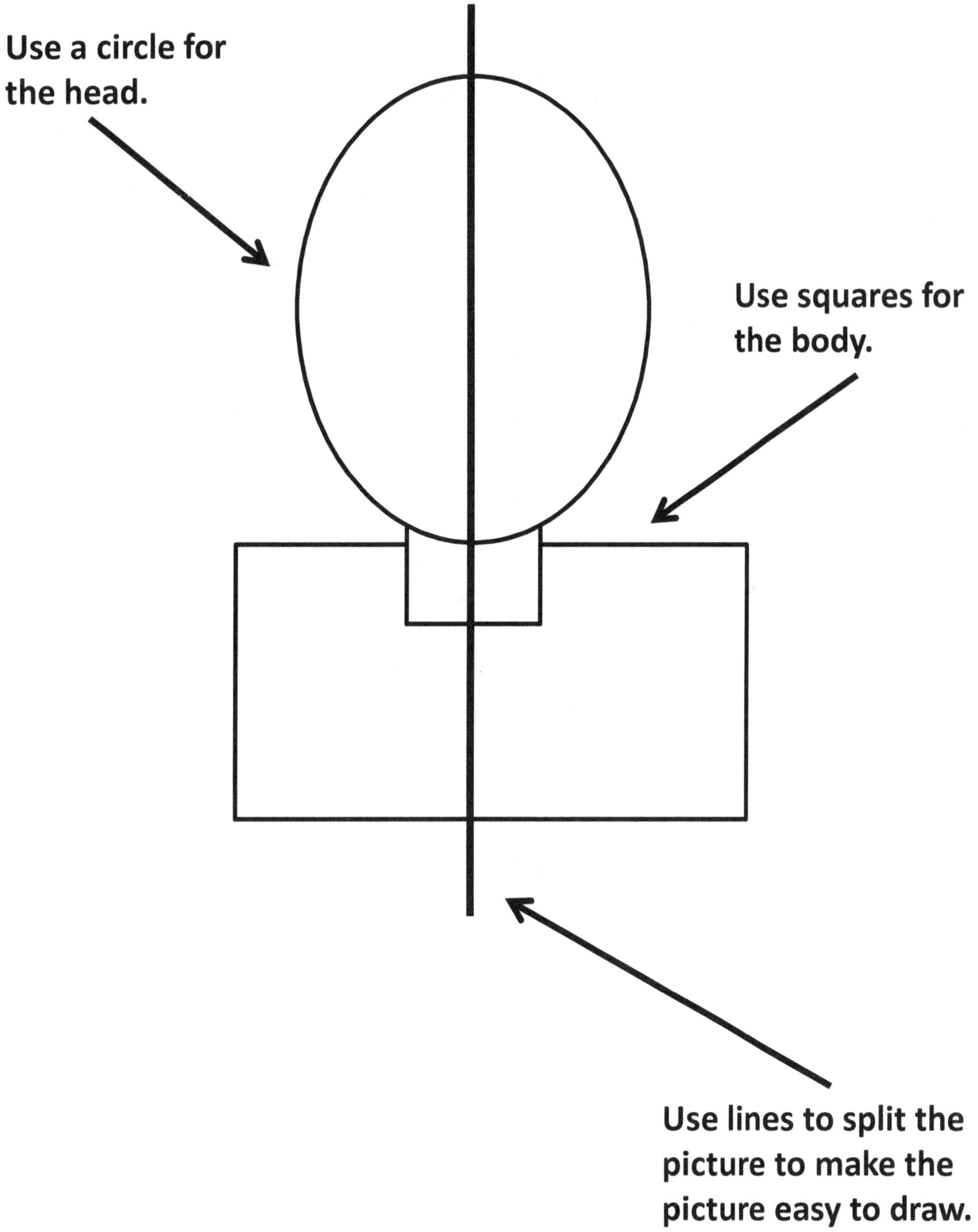
Use a circle for the head.
Use squares for the body.
Use lines to split the picture to make the picture easy to draw.

Erase lines as you create the body.

Shade the square and create the body.

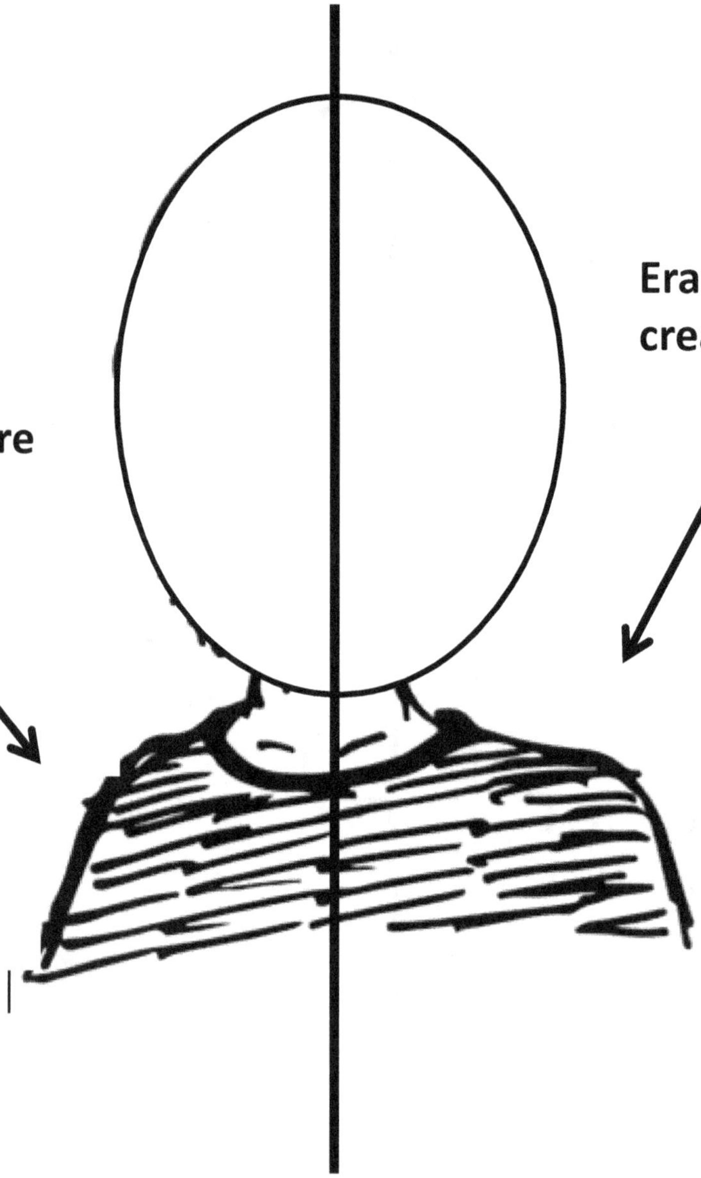

Shade in the hair and beard inside the circle.

Create the nose,
brows and eyes.

FINAL DRAWING

DRAW/SKETCH

DRAW/SKETCH

DRAW/SKETCH

DRAW/SKETCH

DRAW/SKETCH

DRAW/SKETCH

DRAW/SKETCH

DRAW/SKETCH

DRAW/SKETCH

DRAW/SKETCH

DRAW/SKETCH

DRAW/SKETCH

DRAW/SKETCH

DRAW/SKETCH

DRAW/SKETCH

DRAW/SKETCH

DRAW/SKETCH

DRAW/SKETCH

DRAW/SKETCH

DRAW/SKETCH

DRAW/SKETCH

DRAW/SKETCH

DRAW/SKETCH

DRAW/SKETCH

DRAW/SKETCH

DRAW/SKETCH

DRAW/SKETCH

DRAW/SKETCH

DRAW/SKETCH

DRAW/SKETCH

DRAW/SKETCH

DRAW/SKETCH

DRAW/SKETCH

DRAW/SKETCH

DRAW/SKETCH

DRAW/SKETCH

DRAW/SKETCH

DRAW/SKETCH

DRAW/SKETCH

www.ingramcontent.com/pod-product-compliance
Lightning Source LLC
Chambersburg PA
CBHW081725100526
44591CB00016B/2503
* 9 7 8 1 9 5 2 5 2 4 1 2 7 *